Smoothie Bowls

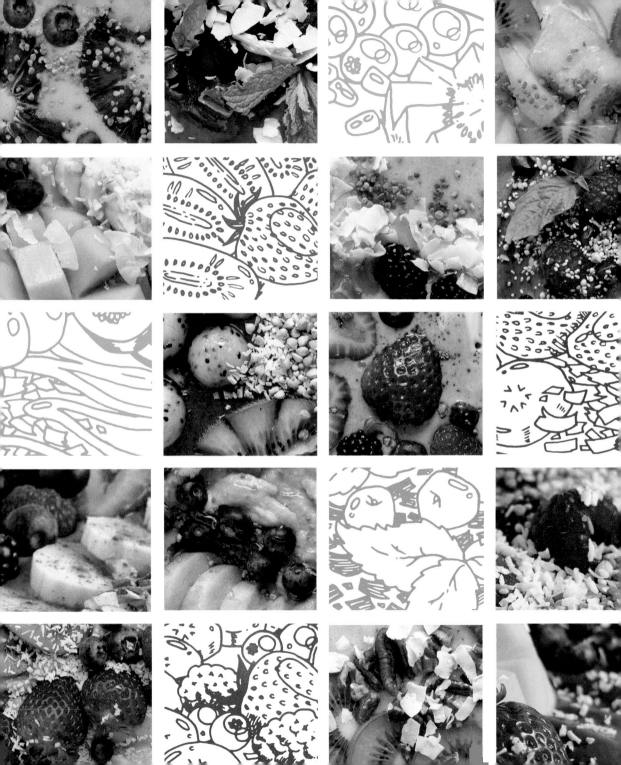

Smoothie Bowls

50 Beautiful, Nutrient-Packed & Satisfying Recipes

MARY WARRINGTON

STERLING EPICURE
New York

STERLING EPICURE
New York

An Imprint of Sterling Publishing Co., Inc.
1166 Avenue of the Americas
New York, NY 10036

ISBN 978-1-4549-2648-1

Distributed in Canada by Sterling Publishing Co., Inc.
c/o Canadian Manda Group, 664 Annette Street
Toronto, Ontario, Canada M6S 2C8
Distributed in the United Kingdom by GMC Distribution Services
Castle Place, 166 High Street, Lewes, East Sussex, England BN7 1XU
Distributed in Australia by NewSouth Books
45 Beach Street, Coogee, NSW 2034, Australia

For information about custom editions, special sales, and premium and corporate purchases, please contact Sterling Special Sales at 800-805-5489 or specialsales@sterlingpublishing.com.

Manufactured in Canada

2 4 6 8 10 9 7 5 3 1

sterlingpublishing.com

Design by Shannon Nicole Plunkett
Illustrations by Sarah Becan

Contents

Introduction

·····································

Smoothie bowls are so much more than just "a smoothie you eat with a spoon"—they're an opportunity to blend flavors, textures, and temperatures while maintaining the healthy components of a typical smoothie. Not only do you get a delicious smoothie as the base of the bowl, but you get toppings—cut-up fruit, drizzled nut butter, flaky coconut, crunchy nuts and seeds—that give each bite a more distinct texture as well as the opportunity for flavor variation bite by bite.

Anatomy of a Smoothie Bowl

A smoothie bowl has three basic parts: the base, the toppings, and the add-ins. The *base* is the carrier—think of it as the ice cream underneath your sundae toppings. This is where the difference between a smoothie and a smoothie bowl becomes apparent: keep the base simple, just enough to taste great and fill up your bowl, but leave some of the more subtle flavor additions for the *toppings*. Toppings are where you can go wild with your imagination—add more or less of any of the toppings I've suggested, and add whatever you think might sound good. Some great toppings include sliced fresh fruit, granola, nuts and seeds, nut butters, edible flowers, ground spices, superfoods, or whatever else you can think of.

While each recipe in this book has the base and the toppings listed out, *add-ins* are something I've mostly omitted. Add-ins are things like protein powder, superfood powders, adaptogens, or any other ingredients that are added less for flavor and more for health benefits. A few examples are maca, flax seeds, spirulina, mushroom powders, and vegetable powders. Most of these impart little to no flavor and should be something you add thoughtfully and purposefully—which is why I haven't dictated when and where to do so. Feel free to use them as you see fit.

Substitutions

You'll find a wide variety of smoothie bowl recipes in this book, and my hope is that you'll use these recipes as a roadmap to create your own. Be adventurous with your substitutions, and feel free to hack these recipes apart. If a recipe calls for coconut milk, but you prefer almond milk: go for it! If you prefer blueberries to raspberries: swap them out! Toppings are a place where you can go especially wild—throw on whatever you want.

An important component of most smoothie bases is one ingredient to add creaminess—most often I call for yogurt or banana, since it's healthy and adds a sweet, creamy element to the smoothie. This is an area that you could easily swap around, but make sure you at least have *something* to introduce a creamy element. Options include the previously mentioned banana or yogurt, as well as zucchini (yes, really!), any milk or milk alternative, avocado, coconut meat, tofu, or even ice cream. Experiment with what works for you and your dietary needs with any of the recipes in this book.

Dairy Alternatives

I call for a number of dairy and dairy alternatives in this book—again, these are interchangeable. One note about *coconut milk* vs. *coconut cream*: When I call for coconut milk, I'm referring to the kind you'll find in the milk section, in a carton. It's quite liquid and meant to be a milk alternative. Coconut cream will likely come in a can or small box, and it is much more viscous and has a higher fat content (this is what you'd use when cooking a curry). For the most part I call for coconut milk, but there are a few recipes in here that call for coconut cream (or both).

Other dairy alternatives include nut milks (cashew, pecan, sunflower, almond, etc.), rice milk, soy milk, sesame milk, and many more. Many of these are also used to make yogurt. You can always make your own, but they should also be readily available in the natural section of your local grocery store.

Equipment

The only required ingredient for this book is a blender. The higher powered it is, the better—especially to maintain a thicker consistency for the base. You will notice, though, that just about all the ingredients for the base of each recipe are listed by weight; having a kitchen scale will make this easy to follow. If you don't have a kitchen scale, you can read the recipes as relative amounts. For example, if I call for 8 ounces of banana, 8 ounces of yogurt, and 4 ounces of strawberries, add equal parts of banana and yogurt, and half as much strawberries. Smoothies are forgiving, so eyeballing isn't a terrible thing to do if you don't have a scale.

Assembly

A major difference between smoothies and smoothie bowls is the consistency of the blended base: a bowl needs to be quite thick in order to suspend the toppings. For that reason, the amount of nonfrozen liquid in each recipe is relatively small. Depending on your blender, you may need to add slightly more than I've called for, but the goal is to add as little as possible.

Here's my workflow when I'm making a smoothie bowl:

1. Assemble all toppings, and prep (chop, measure, etc.) as needed.

2. Assemble all base ingredients, blend to as thick of a mixture as I can.

3. Pour the base into a bowl, and immediately top with the prepared toppings.

4. Eat!

Prep Tips

To make a great smoothie bowl, you'll need to have the right ingredients on hand and prepped. Many of the recipes in this book call for frozen cubes of liquid—juice, milk, yogurt, coconut water, etc. This takes a little bit of planning ahead. I use silicone ice cube trays (they're easy to use and clean) to freeze liquids and yogurts—just freeze and then transfer to freezer-safe resealable bags. I chop fruit into small pieces, lay them in a single layer on a baking sheet to freeze, and then transfer the frozen fruit to freezer-safe resealable bags.

Freezing is also a great way to always have greens on hand. I put handfuls of spinach or kale in my food processor with a few tablespoons of water, process until pretty smooth, and then freeze in ice cube trays. This means I don't have to worry about my greens going bad in the refrigerator before I get to them.

Recipes in this book list frozen ingredients as such. If frozen is not specified in the ingredients list, use fresh. Many of the recipes call for "mixed seeds"; the combination is up to you. I use a mixture of chia, flax, quinoa, sprouted millet and buckwheat, hemp, and amaranth, or any other seeds I have on hand at the time. Recipes calling for mixed seeds list them in measurements of teaspoons rather than ounces.

Assemble all ingredients

Separate out the topping ingredients
from the base ingredients

Do the prep work for the toppings
(chopping, shredding, peeling, etc)
and set them aside

Blend the base!

Pour the base evenly
into a bowl

Immediately arrange
toppings on the base

Serve
and enjoy!

Recipes

···

The following recipes are a starting point for you to jump into the world of making smoothie bowls! They span a range of flavors from sweet to sour to spicy to rich to tangy—you get the idea! Use them as guides to get ratios and textures right, get your inspiration flowing, and maybe try some ingredients that are new to you. **Enjoy!**

DIETARY INFO

Each recipe is labeled, letting you know if it's vegan (v), gluten-free (gf), or dairy free (df). If it has none of the labels, it's because none apply! If you have dietary restrictions and are comfortable making substitutions (dairy-free milk for cow's milk, for example), go right ahead!

Raspberry Basil Pomegranate

v/gf/df

This gorgeous bowl is ripe with tangy fruit—pomegranate doing the heavy lifting, supported by raspberries and apple, along with banana to smooth it all out. Basil brings a fresh floral quality, and unusual flavor that takes this bowl the extra mile.

Yield: 1 Smoothie Bowl

BASE

8 ounces frozen banana
8 ounces frozen raspberries
4 ounces apple slices
$\frac{1}{8}$ cup packed fresh basil leaves
4 ounces pomegranate juice

TOPPINGS

1 ounce pomegranate arils
1 ounce raspberries
1 teaspoon mixed seeds (see Prep Tips, page x)
Fresh basil leaves, for garnish

INSTRUCTIONS

1. Add the frozen banana, frozen raspberries, apple slices, basil leaves, and pomegranate juice to the blender.

2. Blend until smooth.

3. Add the base to a bowl and arrange the pomegranate arils, raspberries, and mixed seeds on top. Garnish with extra basil.

Honey Ginger Peach

Honey, yogurt, and peach blend together for a smooth and comforting bowl. Add the ginger and this bowl becomes a fun, zesty mix of flavors! Bee pollen and fresh fruit as toppings help this recipe shine as a healthy, refreshing smoothie bowl.

Yield: 1 Smoothie Bowl

BASE

8 ounces frozen plain yogurt cubes

1 tablespoon honey

1 tablespoon chopped fresh ginger

12 ounces frozen peaches

4 ounces orange juice

TOPPINGS

2 ounces peach slices

1 ounce blueberries

1 teaspoon honey

1 teaspoon bee pollen

INSTRUCTIONS

1. Add the frozen yogurt, honey, ginger, frozen peaches, and orange juice to the blender.

2. Blend until smooth.

3. Add the base to a bowl and arrange peach slices and blueberries on top. Drizzle with honey and sprinkle bee pollen over the other toppings.

Coco Berry

v/gf/df

Coconut milk and almond butter provide a rich, smooth texture and mix well with tangy berries and sweet banana. Coconut flakes, berries, and drizzled almond butter finish it with a nutty mix of textures.

Yield: 1 Smoothie Bowl

BASE

4 ounces frozen coconut water cubes

8 ounces frozen coconut milk cubes

8 ounces frozen mixed berries

4 ounces coconut water

TOPPINGS

1 tablespoon dried coconut flakes

2 ounces berries

¼ banana, sliced

1 teaspoon almond butter

INSTRUCTIONS

1. Add the frozen coconut water, frozen coconut milk, frozen mixed berries, and coconut water to the blender.

2. Blend until smooth.

3. Add the base to a bowl, sprinkle with dried coconut flakes, and arrange the berries and banana on top. Drizzle with the almond butter.

Mango Lassi

gf

A simple mango lassi gets an upgrade with toppings for this bowl. The base is deliciously creamy mango, and a variety of fruit toppings bring fun texture and complementary flavors. Try adding a ¼ teaspoon of ground cardamom to the base for an entirely different experience!

Yield: 1 Smoothie Bowl

BASE

10 ounces frozen mango slices

8 ounces frozen plain yogurt cubes

4 ounces milk

1 date, pitted

TOPPINGS

¼ banana, sliced

1 ounce mango cubes

1 ounce blueberries

1 teaspoon dried coconut flakes

INSTRUCTIONS

1. Add the frozen mango, frozen yogurt, milk, and date to the blender.

2. Blend until smooth.

3. Add the base to a bowl and arrange the banana, mangos, and blueberries on top. Sprinkle dried coconut flakes over the other toppings.

Pumpkin Pie

Indulge in this pumpkin pie bowl while keeping up your healthy habits. Pumpkin pie spices shine in this recipe, bringing the creamy yogurt and pumpkin puree together perfectly. For a healthier topping, swap the shortbread for toasted pecans!

Yield: 1 Smoothie Bowl

BASE

6 ounces pumpkin puree

8 ounces frozen vanilla yogurt cubes

8 ounces frozen banana

$\frac{1}{2}$ teaspoon ground cinnamon

$\frac{1}{8}$ teaspoon ground ginger

$\frac{1}{8}$ teaspoon ground nutmeg

Pinch of ground cloves

2 ounces carrot juice

TOPPINGS

1 ounce crumbled shortbread cookies

2 tablespoons vanilla yogurt

INSTRUCTIONS

1. Add the pumpkin puree, frozen yogurt, and frozen banana to the blender. Add the spices and pour in the carrot juice.

2. Blend until smooth.

3. Add the base to a bowl, sprinkle the cookies on top, and finish with swirls of vanilla yogurt.

Citrus Honey

This citrus-forward bowl is mellowed by vanilla yogurt and honey—making it sweet, smooth, and full of tangy citrus flavor. Top this one with as many berries and honey drizzles as you want—it's a great base for playing with toppings!

Yield: 1 Smoothie Bowl

BASE

8 ounces frozen vanilla yogurt
cubes
8 ounces frozen banana
4 ounces frozen orange juice
cubes
1 tablespoon honey
4 ounces grapefruit juice

TOPPINGS

2 ounces grapefruit segments
3 blackberries
1 teaspoon dried coconut flakes
1 teaspoon bee pollen
1 teaspoon honey

INSTRUCTIONS

1. Add the frozen yogurt, frozen banana, frozen orange juice, honey, and grapefruit juice to the blender.

2. Blend until smooth.

3. Add the base to a bowl and arrange the grapefruit and blackberries on top. Sprinkle with dried coconut flakes and bee pollen and drizzle with honey.

Tropical

v/gf/df

In this classic tropical bowl, banana, pineapple, and mango are complemented by coconut water and passionfruit juice to create a sweet and tangy fusion. The date adds sweetness while the fruit and coconut flakes bring a bright flair of color on top.

Yield: 1 Smoothie Bowl

BASE

8 ounces frozen banana
4 ounces frozen pineapple
4 ounces frozen mango
4 ounces frozen coconut water
1 date, pitted
4 ounces passionfruit juice

TOPPINGS

2 ounces mango slices
3 strawberries
¼ banana, sliced
1 teaspoon dried coconut flakes

INSTRUCTIONS

1. Add the frozen banana, frozen pineapple, frozen mango, frozen coconut water, date, and passionfruit juice to the blender.

2. Blend until smooth.

3. Add the base to a bowl and arrange the mango slices, strawberries, and banana on top. Sprinkle with coconut flakes.

Chocolate Peanut Butter

gf

Yogurt and peanut butter bring this bowl a high protein content, while the chocolate gives it the feeling of indulgence. Zucchini serves as a banana replacement—adding a creamy quality without much flavor, and bringing tons of nutrients as well. Load on the toppings here—doesn't anything taste great with peanut butter?

Yield: 1 Smoothie Bowl

BASE

8 ounces frozen vanilla yogurt cubes

6 ounces frozen zucchini

2 tablespoons cacao nibs (or dark chocolate)

1 tablespoon peanut butter

2 dates, pitted

4 ounces milk

TOPPINGS

2 teaspoons peanut butter

1 teaspoon cacao nibs

3 strawberries

INSTRUCTIONS

1. Add the frozen yogurt, frozen zucchini, cacao nibs, peanut butter, dates, and milk to the blender.

2. Blend until smooth.

3. Add the base to a bowl and arrange peanut butter, cocoa nibs, and strawberries on top.

Strawberry Kiwi

v/gf/df

The classic pairing of strawberry and kiwi come together for a bright, fresh bowl ready to wake up your taste buds. Top this one with colorful fruits, nuts, and seeds for a filling meal with varying textures.

Yield: 1 Smoothie Bowl

BASE

8 ounces frozen banana
6 ounces frozen kiwi
6 ounces frozen strawberries
4 ounces orange juice
1 date, pitted

TOPPINGS

3 strawberries
$\frac{1}{2}$ kiwi, sliced
1 teaspoon sliced almonds
1 teaspoon mixed seeds
  (see Prep Tips, page x)

INSTRUCTIONS

1. Add the frozen banana, frozen kiwi, frozen strawberries, orange juice, and date to the blender.

2. Blend until smooth.

3. Add the base to a bowl and arrange the strawberries and kiwi on top. Sprinkle almonds and mixed seeds over the other toppings.

Almond Butter Kale Berry

v/gf/df

Almond butter and hemp hearts bring a protein punch to this healthy kale and berry smoothie bowl. This bowl is a great go-to for an easy, everyday source of greens and fruit.

Yield: 1 Smoothie Bowl

BASE

8 ounces frozen mixed berries
8 ounces frozen banana
1 tablespoon almond butter
1 cup packed kale leaves
4 ounces almond milk

TOPPINGS

2 ounces berries
1 tablespoon hemp hearts
1 teaspoon almond butter
1 teaspoon sliced almonds

INSTRUCTIONS

1. Add the frozen berries, frozen banana, almond butter, kale, and almond milk to the blender.

2. Blend until smooth.

3. Add the base to a bowl and arrange the berries and hemp hearts on top. Drizzle with almond butter and sprinkle sliced almonds over the other toppings.

Chili Mango

v/gf/df

Chili mango brings a spicy kick to what would be a mellow, creamy bowl—an ode to Southeast Asia, where snacks of mango sprinkled with chili can often be found! Sweet, ripe mangoes hold their own against the paprika, making an unusual spicy bowl.

Yield: 1 Smoothie Bowl

BASE

8 ounces frozen mango

4 ounces frozen banana

8 ounces frozen coconut milk cubes

½ teaspoon paprika

4 ounces coconut milk

TOPPINGS

2 ounces sliced mango

2 dates, pitted and chopped

2 teaspoons dried coconut flakes

Light dusting of paprika

INSTRUCTIONS

1. Add the frozen mango, frozen banana, frozen coconut milk cubes, paprika, and coconut milk to the blender.

2. Blend until smooth.

3. Add the base to a bowl and arrange the mango and dates on top. Sprinkle with dried coconut flakes and dust with paprika.

Vitamin C Boost

v/gf/df

While oranges are usually touted as the top source of vitamin C, there are actually plenty of other fruits and vegetables that have higher levels of this immune-supporting vitamin. Tropical fruits blend with healthy kale and cranberry juice for a bowl that'll kick that cold in no time. This is a great bowl to mix in adaptogens or other health boosters for a total tune up.

Yield: 1 Smoothie Bowl

BASE

1 cup packed kale leaves
8 ounces frozen orange juice cubes
8 ounces frozen strawberries
4 ounces frozen mango
1 teaspoon maca
4 ounces cranberry juice

TOPPINGS

3 strawberries
1 kiwi, sliced
2 ounces mango cubes

INSTRUCTIONS

1. Add the kale, frozen orange juice, frozen strawberries, frozen mango, maca, and cranberry juice to the blender.

2. Blend until smooth.

3. Add the base to a bowl and arrange the strawberries, kiwi, and mango on top.

Blood Orange Bee Pollen

gf

Blood orange and sweet bee pollen combine for a sweet-tart flavor in this bowl. If you can't find blood orange juice in the store, make your own by squeezing fresh blood oranges (or use slices of fresh blood orange for added fiber!). Add some crunch to this colorful bowl with some mixed seeds or nuts as extra toppings!

Yield: 1 Smoothie Bowl

BASE

8 ounces frozen vanilla yogurt cubes

4 ounces frozen banana

4 ounces frozen orange juice cubes

6 ounces blood orange juice

TOPPINGS

2 ounces blood orange slices

1 ounce blueberries

½ kiwi

1 teaspoon bee pollen

INSTRUCTIONS

1. Add the frozen yogurt, frozen banana, frozen orange juice, and blood orange juice to the blender.

2. Blend until smooth.

3. Add the base to a bowl and arrange the blood orange slices, blueberries, and kiwi on top. Sprinkle with bee pollen.

Peach Chia Kale

v/gf/df

Nutritious kale is almost hidden behind bold pineapple and peach flavors in this bowl. Creamy coconut milk helps smooth everything out, and chia seeds give a superfood punch and keep you full longer. Use your favorite granola on top of this bright, summery bowl!

Yield: 1 Smoothie Bowl

BASE

1 cup packed kale leaves

8 ounces frozen coconut milk cubes

8 ounces frozen peach cubes

4 ounces pineapple juice

1 teaspoon chia seeds

TOPPINGS

2 ounces peach slices

¼ banana, sliced

1 teaspoon chia seeds

1 tablespoon granola

INSTRUCTIONS

1. Add the kale, frozen coconut milk, frozen peaches, pineapple juice, and chia seeds to the blender.

2. Blend until smooth.

3. Add the base to a bowl and arrange peaches and banana on top. Sprinkle chia seeds and granola over the other toppings.

Dragon Fruit Cashew Coconut

v/gf/df

The base for this bowl is simple: nut milks and dragon fruit—a colorful fruit found predominantly in southeast Asia. The mild flavors of the base give the toppings more room to shine. Coconut and mixed seeds add nuttiness and crunch, while more dragon fruit and kiwi give color and sweetness. Feel free to pile on the fruit toppings here—mango and papaya would be great additions.

Yield: 1 Smoothie Bowl

BASE

8 ounces frozen dragon fruit

8 ounces frozen cashew
   milk cubes

4 ounces frozen coconut
   milk cubes

4 ounces cashew milk

TOPPINGS

2 ounces dragon fruit, sliced

½ kiwi, sliced

1 teaspoon shredded dried
   coconut

1 teaspoon mixed seeds
   (see Prep Tips, page x)

INSTRUCTIONS

1. Add the frozen dragon fruit, frozen cashew milk, frozen coconut milk, and cashew milk to the blender.

2. Blend until smooth.

3. Add the base to a bowl and arrange the dragon fruit and kiwi on top. Sprinkle with coconut and mixed seeds.

Citrus Berry

Sweet berries and tangy citrus are a perfect match in this brightly colored bowl. Slice the citrus into beautiful shapes before arranging on the top of this bowl, and enjoy their contrast with the sweet drizzle of honey!

Yield: 1 Smoothie Bowl

BASE

8 ounces frozen banana

4 ounces frozen vanilla yogurt cubes

8 ounces frozen mixed berries

4 ounces orange juice

TOPPINGS

2 ounces sliced grapefruit

2 ounces berries

2 ounces sliced blood orange

1 teaspoon chia seeds

1 teaspoon honey

INSTRUCTIONS

1. Add the frozen banana, frozen yogurt, frozen mixed berries, and orange juice to the blender.

2. Blend until smooth.

3. Add the base to a bowl and arrange grapefruit, berries, and blood orange slices on top. Sprinkle with chia seeds and drizzle honey over the other toppings.

Peanut Butter Banana

This filling bowl is high in protein and flavor. Think of it as a smoothie bowl version of peanut butter oatmeal—oats, peanut butter, banana, and creamy yogurt. Topped with some granola, it's a hearty meal to stick with you all day.

Yield: 1 Smoothie Bowl

BASE

8 ounces frozen banana

6 ounces frozen vanilla yogurt cubes

1 tablespoon raw oats

2 tablespoons peanut butter

6 ounces milk

TOPPINGS

¼ banana, sliced

2 ounces granola

1 tablespoon peanut butter

INSTRUCTIONS

1. Add the frozen banana, frozen yogurt, oats, peanut butter, and milk to the blender.

2. Blend until smooth.

3. Add the base to a bowl and arrange the banana slices on top. Sprinkle with granola and drizzle peanut butter over the other toppings.

Grapefruit Macadamia

v/gf/df

Macadamia milk is easily found in a natural food market but rarely used in smoothie making. This deliciously smooth nut milk gives a new, alternative flavor that pairs well with sour grapefruit. The dates in this bowl keep it sweet enough to enjoy, as does the honey drizzled on top. Blackberries on top work well with the grapefruit, and fresh macadamia nuts bring a lovely crunch!

Yield: 1 Smoothie Bowl

BASE

6 ounces frozen macadamia
milk cubes
6 ounces frozen banana
4 ounces frozen grapefruit
juice cubes
2 dates, pitted
8 ounces grapefruit juice

TOPPINGS

2 ounces grapefruit
2 ounces blackberries
1 tablespoon chopped
macadamia nuts
1 teaspoon bee pollen
1 teaspoon honey

INSTRUCTIONS

1. Add the frozen macadamia milk, frozen banana, frozen grapefruit juice, dates, and grapefruit juice to the blender.

2. Blend until smooth.

3. Add the base to a bowl and arrange the grapefruit, blackberries, and macadamia nuts on top. Sprinkle with bee pollen and drizzle with honey.

Banana Almond Date

v/gf/df

This superfood smoothie bowl almost feels like ice cream. While it relies mainly on frozen banana, the dates sweeten the bowl while giving almond and cinnamon the opportunity to shine through with flavor. Top this bowl with colorful berries and nuts.

Yield: 1 Smoothie Bowl

BASE

12 ounces frozen banana

8 ounces frozen almond milk cubes

2 dates, pitted

$\frac{1}{2}$ teaspoon cinnamon

1 teaspoon maca

4 ounces almond milk

TOPPINGS

$\frac{1}{4}$ banana, sliced

3 strawberries

1 tablespoon toasted pecans

1 teaspoon shredded dried coconut

INSTRUCTIONS

1. Add the frozen banana, frozen almond milk, dates, cinnamon, maca, and almond milk to the blender.

2. Blend until smooth.

3. Add the base to a bowl and arrange the banana, strawberries, and pecans on top. Sprinkle with shredded dried coconut.

Strawberry Spirulina

The classic strawberry and banana combination gets a superfood boost with spirulina, all while remaining tangy thanks to the orange juice, and smooth thanks to the yogurt. Topped with more fruit and nuts, this healthy bowl is satisfying as well as full of nutrients.

Yield: 1 Smoothie Bowl

BASE

8 ounces frozen strawberries

4 ounces frozen banana

8 ounces frozen vanilla yogurt cubes

1 tablespoon spirulina powder

4 ounces orange juice

TOPPINGS

3 strawberries

2 ounces orange slices

1 tablespoon sliced almonds

INSTRUCTIONS

1. Add the frozen strawberries, frozen banana, frozen yogurt, spirulina, and orange juice to the blender.

2. Blend until smooth.

3. Add the base to a bowl and arrange the strawberries and orange slices on top. Sprinkle with sliced almonds.

Blueberry Cashew Chia

v/df

Cashew milk keeps this bowl buttery smooth, and blueberries bring an antioxidant boost along with their delicious flavor. Chia seeds add an additional superfood boost to keep you full, hydrated, and healthy. Easily make this bowl gluten-free by omitting the granola and using more nuts.

Yield: 1 Smoothie Bowl

BASE

8 ounces frozen cashew milk cubes
4 ounces frozen banana
8 ounces frozen blueberries
1 teaspoon chia seeds
6 ounces cashew milk

TOPPINGS

1 ounce blueberries
2 strawberries
½ ounce chopped cashews
1 teaspoon chia seeds
1 tablespoon granola

INSTRUCTIONS

1. Add the frozen cashew milk, frozen banana, frozen blueberries, chia seeds, and cashew milk to the blender.

2. Blend until smooth.

3. Add the base to a bowl and arrange the blueberries, strawberries, and cashews on top. Sprinkle with chia seeds and granola.

Golden Milk

Anti-inflammatory turmeric is the star of this golden bowl. The earthy flavor can be an acquired taste for some, but mixed with dates, yogurt, banana, and cashew milk, it's easy to introduce in a tasty way. Along with other toppings, the berries help sweeten and familiarize the turmeric base.

Yield: 1 Smoothie Bowl

BASE

8 ounces frozen vanilla yogurt
   cubes
8 ounces frozen banana
1 teaspoon ground turmeric
3 dates, pitted
4 ounces cashew milk

TOPPINGS

2 ounces berries
1 teaspoon mixed seeds
   (see Prep Tips, page x)
1 teaspoon bee pollen
1 teaspoon shredded dried
   coconut

INSTRUCTIONS

1. Add the frozen yogurt, frozen banana, turmeric, dates, and cashew milk to the blender.

2. Blend until smooth.

3. Add the base to a bowl and arrange the berries on top. Sprinkle with seeds, bee pollen, and shredded coconut.

Cherry Coconut Beet

This bowl is packed full of colorful, rich flavors. From sweet carrot juice and dates, to luscious coconut cream, to nutritious beets and juicy cherries, this bowl packs a punch. Add some texture with seeds and coconut on top.

Yield: 1 Smoothie Bowl

BASE

4 ounces cooked, cooled
   beets
8 ounces frozen coconut milk
   cubes
4 ounces frozen cherries
2 dates, pitted
2 ounces coconut cream
4 ounces carrot juice

TOPPINGS

2 ounces pear slices
1 teaspoon mixed seeds
   (see Prep Tips, page x)
1 tablespoon shredded dried
   coconut
1 teaspoon vanilla yogurt

INSTRUCTIONS

1. Add the beets, frozen coconut milk, frozen cherries, dates, coconut cream, and carrot juice to the blender.

2. Blend until smooth.

3. Add the base to a bowl and arrange the pear slices on top. Sprinkle with mixed seeds and coconut and drizzle with yogurt.

Raspberry Chia

gf

This smoothie bowl is a raspberry lover's dream! This bowl is high on tangy raspberry flavor, with a raspberry-heavy base and raspberries on top. Chia and dried coconut flakes add more texture to this bright pink bowl.

Yield: 1 Smoothie Bowl

BASE
8 ounces frozen raspberries
8 ounces frozen banana
4 ounces vanilla yogurt
$\frac{1}{4}$ cup coconut water

TOPPINGS
2 ounces raspberries
1 tablespoon dried coconut
　　flakes
1 teaspoon chia seeds

INSTRUCTIONS

1. Add the frozen raspberries, frozen banana, yogurt, and coconut water to the blender.

2. Blend until smooth.

3. Add the base to a bowl and arrange the raspberries on top. Sprinkle with dried coconut flakes and chia seeds.

Banana Bread

Date-sweetened banana reaches new levels with the spices in this bowl—it's like fresh-baked banana bread in smoothie form. The toppings for this bowl are reminiscent of things you might find in banana bread—nuts, nut butter, berries, and more banana. If you're feeling especially decadent, you could even throw in some chocolate chips.

Yield: 1 Smoothie Bowl

BASE

12 ounces frozen banana

6 ounces frozen vanilla yogurt cubes

½ teaspoon cinnamon

1 pinch nutmeg

2 dates, pitted

4 ounces vanilla yogurt

TOPPINGS

½ banana

3 strawberries

1 tablespoon toasted pecans

1 teaspoon almond butter

Sprinkle of cinnamon

INSTRUCTIONS

1. Add the frozen banana, frozen yogurt, cinnamon, nutmeg, dates, and yogurt to the blender.

2. Blend until smooth.

3. Add the base to a bowl and arrange the banana, strawberries, and pecans on top. Drizzle with almond butter and dust with cinnamon.

Coconut Kiwi Nut

v/gf/df

This mild base creates a canvas for toppings to go wild. The kiwi is subtle and mellowed by creamy banana and coconut milk, giving the toppings more room to shine. Try adding other tropical fruits or a drizzle of your favorite nut butter.

Yield: 1 Smoothie Bowl

BASE

6 ounces frozen coconut milk cubes

8 ounces frozen banana

6 ounces frozen kiwi fruit

6 ounces coconut milk

TOPPINGS

1 kiwi, sliced

1 tablespoon toasted nuts (pecans, almonds, cashews)

2 ounces raspberries

1 tablespoon dried coconut flakes

INSTRUCTIONS

1. Add the frozen coconut milk, frozen banana, frozen kiwi, and coconut milk to the blender.

2. Blend until smooth.

3. Add the base to a bowl and arrange the kiwi, toasted nuts, and raspberries on top. Sprinkle with coconut flakes.

Chocolate Almond Chia

Cacao and almond come together for a decadent treat in a smoothie bowl. Topped with crunchy cacao, almond, and pomegranate, this bowl is heavy on texture.

Yield: 1 Smoothie Bowl

BASE

8 ounces frozen almond milk
  cubes
8 ounces frozen vanilla
  yogurt cubes
2 ounces cacao nibs
  (or dark chocolate)
8 ounces almond milk

TOPPINGS

1 teaspoon chia seeds
1 tablespoon chopped
  cacao nibs
1 tablespoon almond slices
1 ounce pomegranate arils

INSTRUCTIONS

1. Add the frozen almond milk, frozen yogurt, cacao nibs, and almond milk to the blender.

2. Blend until smooth.

3. Add the base to a bowl and sprinkle with chia seeds, cacao nibs, almonds, and pomegranate arils.

Spiced Persimmon Apple

gf

Warm winter flavors come together in this smoothie bowl with persimmon, ginger, spices, and toasted pecans—among others. When tropical flavors are hard to find, or you just feel like a seasonal winter bowl, this one is for you!

Yield: 1 Smoothie Bowl

BASE

8 ounces apple chunks

4 ounces frozen persimmon

8 ounces frozen vanilla yogurt cubes

1/4 teaspoon cinnamon

1 pinch nutmeg

1 teaspoon ginger

4 ounces apple juice

TOPPINGS

1/2 persimmon, sliced

2 ounces sliced apple

1 tablespoon toasted pecans

1 teaspoon vanilla yogurt

Dusting of cinnamon

INSTRUCTIONS

1. Add the apple, frozen persimmon, frozen yogurt, cinnamon, nutmeg, ginger, and apple juice to the blender.

2. Blend until smooth.

3. Add the base to a bowl and arrange the persimmon, apple, and pecans on top. Drizzle with yogurt and dust with cinnamon.

Watermelon Cucumber

v/gf/df

Watermelon and cucumber come together for a refreshing, summery bowl low on creaminess and high on hydration. Toppings of cherries and mint give an extra punch of revitalizing summer flavor.

Yield: 1 Smoothie Bowl

BASE

8 ounces frozen watermelon cubes

8 ounces frozen cucumber cubes

4 ounces frozen coconut water cubes

4 ounces coconut water

TOPPINGS

2 ounces watermelon cubes

2 ounces cherries

5 fresh mint leaves

INSTRUCTIONS

1. Add the frozen watermelon, frozen cucumber, frozen coconut water, and coconut water to the blender.

2. Blend until smooth.

3. Add the base to a bowl and arrange the watermelon and cherries on top. Garnish with mint.

Black Sesame Cherry

gf

Black sesame seeds give this unconventional bowl a mild nutty flavor, which balances nicely with the sweet fruity cherry and creamy banana and yogurt. Simple toppings prevent distraction from the subtle black sesame flavor.

Yield: 1 Smoothie Bowl

BASE

8 ounces frozen vanilla yogurt
   cubes
6 ounces frozen banana
6 ounces frozen cherries
1 tablespoon black sesame
   seeds
4 ounces carrot
   (or pomegranate) juice

TOPPINGS

2 ounces cherries
1 teaspoon black sesame seeds

INSTRUCTIONS

1. Add the frozen yogurt, frozen banana, frozen cherries, black sesame seeds, and carrot juice to the blender.

2. Blend until smooth.

3. Add the base to a bowl and arrange the cherries on top. Sprinkle with more sesame seeds.

Zucchini Oat Acai

v/df

Superfood acai gets a hearty makeover with the addition of oats and zucchini—a creamy alternative to banana. With even more berries, oats, and chia on top, this bowl will keep you full of energy!

Yield: 1 Smoothie Bowl

BASE

8 ounces frozen zucchini

8 ounces frozen coconut milk cubes

4 ounces frozen acai berries

1 tablespoon uncooked oats

4 ounces acai juice

TOPPINGS

¼ banana, sliced

1 tablespoon uncooked oats

1 ounce acai berries

½ teaspoon chia seeds

INSTRUCTIONS

1. Add the frozen zucchini, frozen coconut milk, frozen acai berries, oats, and acai juice to the blender.

2. Blend until smooth.

3. Add the base to a bowl and the arrange the banana, oats, and acai berries on top. Sprinkle with chia seeds.

Creamy Honey Pineapple

gf

To say this bowl is creamy is an understatement—it's smooth, sweet, tart, and oh-so-enjoyable. Acidic pineapple is mellowed by yogurt, sweetened by honey, and topped with flavorful bee pollen.

Yield: 1 Smoothie Bowl

BASE
8 ounces frozen pineapple
8 ounces frozen vanilla yogurt
4 ounces frozen banana
2 tablespoons honey
4 ounces pineapple juice

TOPPINGS
1 ounce pineapple cubes
$\frac{1}{2}$ kiwi, sliced
1 teaspoon bee pollen
1 teaspoon honey

INSTRUCTIONS

1. Add the frozen pineapple, frozen yogurt, frozen banana, honey, and pineapple juice to the blender.

2. Blend until smooth.

3. Add the base to a bowl and arrange the pineapple and kiwi on top. Sprinkle with bee pollen and drizzle with honey.

Coconut Blackberry Kiwi

v/gf/df

The contrast in this bowl between dark blackberries and bright kiwi and coconut make for a delicious combination. The base is smooth and creamy, while retaining plenty of flavor from the fruits, and the matching toppings highlight the berry and kiwi flavors even more.

Yield: 1 Smoothie Bowl

BASE

4 ounces frozen coconut
   cream cubes
8 ounces frozen banana
8 ounces frozen blackberries
4 ounces kiwi
4 ounces coconut milk

TOPPINGS

½ kiwi, sliced
2 ounces blackberries
1 teaspoon dried coconut flakes
1 teaspoon honey

INSTRUCTIONS

1. Add the frozen coconut cream, frozen banana, frozen blackberries, kiwi, and coconut milk to the blender.

2. Blend until smooth.

3. Add the base to a bowl and arrange the kiwi and blackberries on top. Sprinkle with coconut and drizzle with honey.

Cherry Coconut

gf

Cherries and coconut work perfectly together in this creamy pink bowl. Chia seeds pack an extra nutritional boost, and sweet dates contrast with the fresh mint.

Yield: 1 Smoothie Bowl

BASE

8 ounces frozen vanilla yogurt cubes

8 ounces frozen cherries

8 ounces coconut water

1 teaspoon chia seeds

TOPPINGS

2 ounces cherries

2 dates, pitted and chopped

1 tablespoon dried coconut flakes

5 fresh mint leaves

INSTRUCTIONS

1. Add the frozen yogurt, frozen cherries, coconut water, and chia seeds to the blender.

2. Blend until smooth.

3. Add the base to a bowl and arrange the cherries and dates on top. Sprinkle with coconut flakes and garnish with mint.

Cranberry Vanilla Maple

Tart cranberries mellow out with vanilla yogurt and banana, while maple syrup gives a natural sweetness to this festive pink bowl. As an unusual flavor for a smoothie, cranberry makes for a fun playground to try various toppings—other fruits, grains, or nuts. For a more decadent topping, try some crumbled pound cake.

Yield: 1 Smoothie Bowl

BASE

8 ounces frozen vanilla yogurt cubes

8 ounces frozen banana

2 tablespoons maple syrup

$\frac{1}{8}$ teaspoon ground vanilla bean

2 ounces cranberries

4 ounces cranberry juice

TOPPINGS

$\frac{1}{2}$ ounce dried cranberries

1 tablespoon granola

1 teaspoon vanilla yogurt

1 teaspoon maple syrup

INSTRUCTIONS

1. Add the frozen yogurt, frozen banana, maple syrup, vanilla bean, cranberries, and cranberry juice to the blender.

2. Blend until smooth.

3. Add the base to a bowl and sprinkle the dried cranberries and granola on top. Drizzle with yogurt and maple syrup.

Mango Spirulina

v/gf/df

This bright green bowl is light and fresh with mango, banana, and coconut water. Spirulina gives it a remarkable shade of green and plenty of nutrients without overpowering the flavor. Fresh fruit and coconut on top keeps the texture interesting.

Yield: 1 Smoothie Bowl

BASE

10 ounces frozen mango

8 ounces frozen banana

4 ounces frozen coconut water cubes

1 tablespoon spirulina powder

4 ounces mango juice

TOPPINGS

1 ounce cubed mango

1 ounce mixed berries

1 teaspoon shredded dried coconut

INSTRUCTIONS

1. Add the frozen mango, frozen banana, frozen coconut water, spirulina, and mango juice to the blender.

2. Blend until smooth.

3. Add the base to a bowl and arrange the fresh mango and berries on top. Sprinkle with coconut flakes.

Dark Chocolate Mint Berry

gf

This dark chocolate bowl still boasts some healthy nutrients with the fabulous pairing of raspberries and mint. Vanilla yogurt and banana give a smooth, creamy base, and the toppings could expand from berries, mint, and chocolate toward any direction you want! Granola or more yogurt would be great alternative, or additional toppings!

Yield: 1 Smoothie Bowl

BASE

4 ounces frozen banana

8 ounces frozen vanilla yogurt cubes

8 ounces frozen raspberries

2 ounces dark chocolate (at least 80 percent)

1 tablespoon fresh mint leaves, chopped

4 ounces cherry juice

TOPPINGS

1 ounce berries

1 teaspoon shaved dark chocolate

5 fresh mint leaves, chopped

INSTRUCTIONS

1. Add the frozen banana, frozen yogurt, frozen raspberries, dark chocolate, mint, and cherry juice to the blender.

2. Blend until smooth.

3. Add the base to a bowl and arrange the berries on top. Sprinkle with shaved chocolate and garnish with mint leaves.

Cinnamon Almond Maca

v/gf/df

Although its flavor is easily confused with a milkshake, this bowl is packed with nutrients. Nutty almond blends with creamy banana, sweet date, and spicy cinnamon for a heavenly mix of smooth flavors.

Yield: 1 Smoothie Bowl

BASE

8 ounces frozen banana

8 ounces frozen almond milk cubes

$\frac{1}{4}$ cup raw almonds

$\frac{1}{2}$ teaspoon cinnamon

2 dates, pitted

1 teaspoon maca

4 ounces almond milk

TOPPINGS

$\frac{1}{4}$ banana, sliced

1 ounce berries

1 teaspoon sliced toasted almonds

Sprinkle of ground cinnamon

INSTRUCTIONS

1. Add the frozen banana, frozen almond milk, almonds, cinnamon, dates, maca, and almond milk to the blender.

2. Blend until smooth.

3. Add the base to a bowl and arrange the banana and berries on top. Sprinkle with sliced almonds and dust with cinnamon.

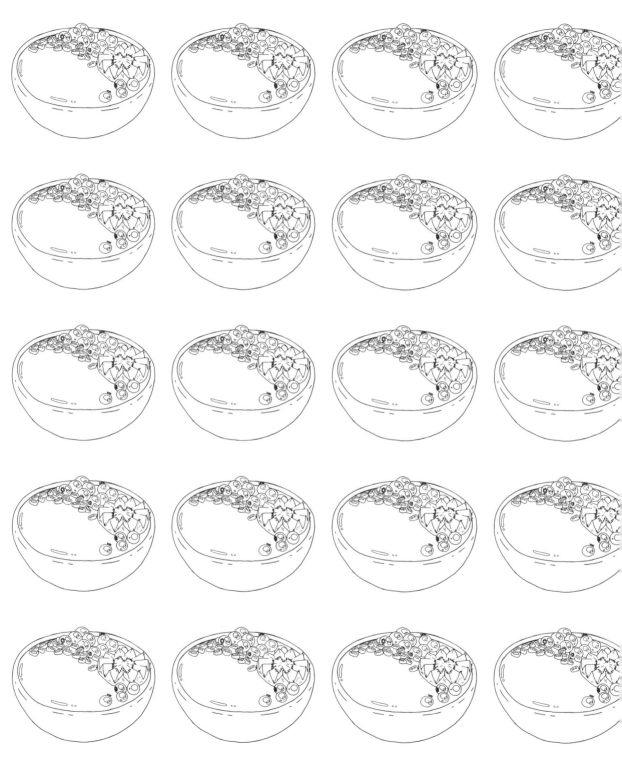

Kiwi Blueberry

This kiwi blueberry bowl keeps it simple with a short ingredient list, but all of them pack a flavor and nutrient punch. Topped with even more fresh fruit, including pomegranate arils for a fun texture, this bowl is nearly all fruit.

Yield: 1 Smoothie Bowl

BASE
8 ounces frozen banana
6 ounces frozen kiwi
6 ounces frozen blueberries
4 ounces coconut water

TOPPINGS
1 ounce blueberries
½ kiwi, sliced
1 ounce pomegranate arils

INSTRUCTIONS

1. Add the frozen banana, frozen kiwi, frozen blueberries, and coconut water to the blender.

2. Blend until smooth.

3. Add the base to a bowl and arrange blueberries, kiwi, and pomegranate arils on top.

Classic Pitaya

v/gf/df

A classic pitaya bowl means tropical flavors and requires pink dragon fruit. This vibrant bowl will catch your attention visually and reward your taste buds with a classic tropical smoothie. Feel free to pile on more tropical fruits to top this beauty.

Yield: 1 Smoothie Bowl

BASE

8 ounces frozen pink
   dragon fruit
4 ounces frozen banana
4 ounces frozen pineapple
4 ounces frozen mango
4 ounces coconut milk

TOPPINGS

2 ounces dragon fruit, pink
   or white, sliced
2 ounces kiwi, sliced

INSTRUCTIONS

1. Add the frozen dragon fruit, frozen banana, frozen pineapple, frozen mango, and coconut milk to the blender.

2. Blend until smooth.

3. Add the base to a bowl and arrange the dragon fruit and kiwi on top.

Creamy Coconut Mango Oat

v/df

This bowl is comforting and filling—oatmeal and coconut cream blend beautifully for a full, hearty bowl. The mango in both the base and the toppings gives it a fresh, fruity profile while remaining deliciously smooth and rich.

Yield: 1 Smoothie Bowl

BASE

8 ounces frozen mango

8 ounces frozen banana

4 ounces canned coconut cream

4 ounces coconut milk

$\frac{1}{8}$ cup raw oats

TOPPINGS

2 ounces sliced mango

1 teaspoon raw oats

1 tablespoon dried coconut flakes

INSTRUCTIONS

1. Add the frozen mango, frozen banana, coconut cream, coconut milk, and oats to the blender.

2. Blend until smooth.

3. Add the base to a bowl and arrange the mango on top. Sprinkle with oats and coconut flakes.

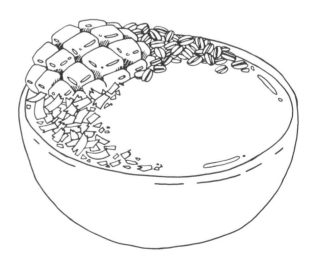

Apple Beet Berry

gf

This bowl packs a nutritious punch with beets, berries, and apple. The apple and berries keep it sweet, while the beets give it a vibrant color and earthy, hearty taste.

Yield: 1 Smoothie Bowl

BASE
4 ounces cooked, cooled beets
8 ounces frozen mixed berries
8 ounces apple
1 tablespoon honey
4 ounces apple juice

TOPPINGS
2 ounces sliced apple
1 ounce mixed berries
1 teaspoon vanilla yogurt

INSTRUCTIONS

1. Add the beets, frozen berries, apple, honey, and apple juice to the blender.

2. Blend until smooth.

3. Add the base to a bowl and arrange the apples and mixed berries on top. Drizzle with yogurt.

Vanilla Matcha

Think of this bowl as a matcha latte in smoothie form—minus the coffee. The matcha flavor comes through in this base, which is topped with creamy vanilla yogurt and fresh berries. This bowl doesn't confuse too many flavors at once, letting you enjoy the unusual flavor of the matcha.

Yield: 1 Smoothie Bowl

BASE

10 ounces frozen vanilla
yogurt cubes

8 ounces frozen banana

2 teaspoons matcha powder

$\frac{1}{4}$ teaspoon ground vanilla
bean

6 ounces milk

TOPPINGS

2 ounces berries

1 tablespoon vanilla yogurt

Sprinkle of matcha powder

INSTRUCTIONS

1. Add the frozen yogurt, frozen banana, matcha, ground vanilla, and milk to the blender.

2. Blend until smooth.

3. Add the base to a bowl and arrange the berries on top. Drizzle with yogurt and dust with matcha powder.

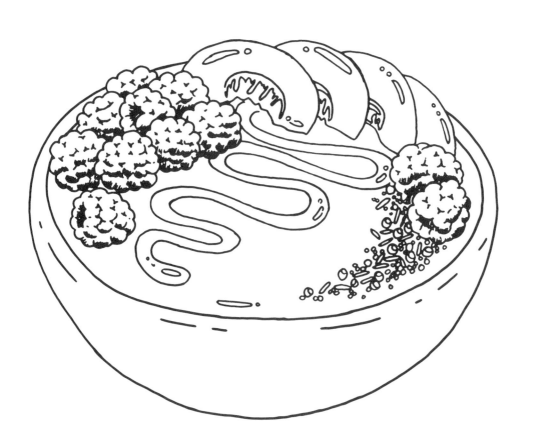

Peach Creamsicle

Peach creamsicle lives up to its name, in bowl form. Frozen peaches become sweet and smooth with yogurt, banana, and honey—plus a slight tangy kick from the orange juice. Topped with more creamy yogurt, it also has texture from fresh raspberries and mixed seeds.

Yield: 1 Smoothie Bowl

BASE

8 ounces frozen vanilla yogurt cubes

8 ounces frozen peach slices

4 ounces frozen banana

4 ounces orange juice

1 teaspoon honey

TOPPINGS

2 ounces peach slices

1 ounce raspberries

1 teaspoon vanilla yogurt

1 teaspoon mixed seeds
   (see Prep Tips, page x)

INSTRUCTIONS

1. Add the frozen yogurt, frozen peaches, frozen banana, orange juice, and honey to the blender.

2. Blend until smooth.

3. Add the base to a bowl and arrange the peaches and raspberries on top. Drizzle with yogurt and sprinkle with mixed seeds.

Tropical Green

v/gf/df

Get your greens with this bowl! Spinach is disguised in flavor, though not in color, by the bold tropical flavors in the base. Toppings continue the tropical theme, with the addition of mixed seeds for crunchy texture.

Yield: 1 Smoothie Bowl

BASE

4 ounces spinach leaves
4 ounces frozen pineapple
4 ounces frozen papaya
4 ounces frozen mango
4 ounces frozen banana
4 ounces orange juice

TOPPINGS

1 ounce sliced mango
1/4 banana, sliced
1 teaspoon mixed seeds
   (see Prep Tips, page x)
1 teaspoon shredded dried
   coconut

INSTRUCTIONS

1. Add the spinach leaves, frozen pineapple, frozen papaya, frozen mango, frozen banana, and orange juice to the blender.

2. Blend until smooth.

3. Add the base to a bowl and arrange the mango and banana on top. Sprinkle with mixed seeds and dried coconut.

Smoothie Bowls • 83

Ginger Pear Beet

Earthy beets gives a healthy base to the other flavors in this bowl—pear, spicy ginger, creamy banana, and sweet carrot juice. With all the nutrients packed into the base, enjoy creamy yogurt and your choice of granola to top this one!

Yield: 1 Smoothie Bowl

BASE

4 ounces cooked, cooled beets

8 ounces frozen pears

8 ounces frozen banana

4 ounces frozen orange juice cubes

1 tablespoon fresh ginger

1 date, pitted

4 ounces carrot juice

TOPPINGS

1 ounce sliced pears

1 tablespoon vanilla yogurt

1 ounce granola

INSTRUCTIONS

1. Add the beets, frozen pears, frozen banana, frozen orange juice, ginger, date, and carrot juice to the blender.

2. Blend until smooth.

3. Add the base to a bowl and arrange the pears on top. Drizzle with yogurt and sprinkle with granola.

Winter Chai

This decadent bowl boasts warm chai spice flavors, smoothed out by vanilla yogurt and banana. Topped with persimmon, cinnamon, and almonds, it's the perfect bowl for winter warming!

Yield: 1 Smoothie Bowl

BASE

8 ounces frozen banana
8 ounces frozen vanilla yogurt
4 ounces frozen chai
    concentrate (see Note)
4 ounces almond milk

TOPPINGS

¼ banana, sliced
½ persimmon, sliced
1 teaspoon almond slices
Sprinkle of cinnamon

INSTRUCTIONS

1. Add the frozen banana, frozen yogurt, frozen chai concentrate, and almond milk to the blender.

2. Blend until smooth.

3. Add the base to a bowl and arrange the banana and persimmon on top. Sprinkle with almond slices and dust with cinnamon.

Note: This can be substituted with dry ground chai spices (cardamom, cinnamon, ginger, cloves, allspice). Make sure to add an additional 4oz of liquid (your choice!) to make up for the loss of volume here.

Coconut Fig

v/gf/df

The base of this bowl is mild, creamy, and nutritious—a great contrast to the vibrant fig and cherry toppings, as well as the bold flavor of maple syrup.

Yield: 1 Smoothie Bowl

BASE

8 ounces frozen coconut milk

8 ounces frozen banana

8 ounces figs

2 ounces coconut cream

TOPPINGS

1 ounce chopped figs

1 ounce cherries

1 teaspoon shredded dried coconut

1 teaspoon maple syrup

INSTRUCTIONS

1. Add the frozen coconut milk, frozen banana, figs, and coconut cream to the blender.

2. Blend until smooth.

3. Add the base to a bowl and arrange the figs and cherries on top. Sprinkle with coconut flakes and drizzle with maple syrup.

Pineapple Avocado Cinnamon

v/gf/df

This creamy bowl introduces a lesser-used smoothie ingredient: avocado! It's smooth, slightly green, and full of tropical flavor. The crunchy macadamia nuts on top add texture.

Yield: 1 Smoothie Bowl

BASE

8 ounces frozen pineapple

4 ounces frozen banana

4 ounces frozen kiwi

$\frac{1}{2}$ teaspoon cinnamon

4 ounces avocado

1 ounce lime juice

4 ounces coconut water

TOPPINGS

2 strawberries

$\frac{1}{2}$ kiwi, sliced

1 tablespoon crushed
   macadamia nuts

Sprinkle of cinnamon

INSTRUCTIONS

1. Add the frozen pineapple, frozen banana, frozen kiwi, cinnamon, avocado, lime juice, and coconut water to the blender.

2. Blend until smooth.

3. Add the base to a bowl and arrange the strawberries, kiwi, and macadamia nuts on top. Dust with cinnamon.

Passionfruit Kiwi Ginger

v/gf/df

Tangy passionfruit and kiwi mix with creamy coconut milk and banana to create a sweet-and-tart combination for this bowl. The ginger kicks in some spice, and the berries on top bring great texture along with a familiar flavor profile against the unusual tropical flavors of the base.

Yield: 1 Smoothie Bowl

BASE

8 ounces frozen banana

8 ounces frozen kiwi

4 ounces frozen coconut milk cubes

2 teaspoons fresh ginger

4 ounces passionfruit juice

TOPPINGS

½ kiwi, sliced

1 ounce berries

1 teaspoon shredded dried coconut

INSTRUCTIONS

1. Add the frozen banana, frozen kiwi, frozen coconut milk, ginger, and passionfruit juice to the blender.

2. Blend until smooth.

3. Add the base to a bowl and arrange the kiwi and berries on top. Sprinkle with dried coconut.